First Facts™

Our Physical World

Color

by Ellen Sturm Niz

Consultant:
Philip W. Hammer, PhD
Vice President, The Franklin Center
The Franklin Institute
Philadelphia, Pennsylvania

Capstone press

Mankato, Minnesota

First Facts is published by Capstone Press,
151 Good Counsel Drive, P.O. Box 669, Mankato, Minnesota 56002.
www.capstonepress.com

Library of Congress Cataloging-in-Publication Data
Niz, Ellen Sturm.
    Color / by Ellen Sturm Niz; consultant, Philip W. Hammer.
    p. cm.—(First facts. Our physical world)
    Includes bibliographical references and index.
    ISBN–13: 978-0-7368-5400-9 (hardcover)
    ISBN–10: 0-7368-5400-2 (hardcover)
    1. Colors—Experiments—Juvenile literature. I. Title. II. Series.
QC495.5.N59 2006
535.6'078—dc22   2005013321

Summary: Introduces young readers to color, its characteristics, and its uses in the world.
    Includes instructions for an activity to demonstrate some of color's characteristics.

Editorial Credits
Aaron Sautter, editor; Linda Clavel, set designer; Bobbi J. Dey, book designer;
    Molly Nei, illustrator; Kelly Garvin, photo researcher/photo editor

Photo Credits
Capstone Press/Gary Sundermeyer, 10; Karon Dubke, cover, 13 (both)
Corbis/Bryan F. Peterson, 6; Matt Brown, 5
Getty Images Inc./Time Life Pictures, 18; Tim Flach, 16
Photodisc, 17, 21
Photo Researchers, Inc./David Parker, 8
SuperStock/Age Fotostock, 9; SuperStock Inc., 20

1 2 3 4 5 6 11 10 09 08 07 06

Table of Contents

Color

Color is all around us. Tulips bloom in red, pink, and yellow. White clouds float through a blue sky. Everywhere you look, color fills our world.

Fun Fact!

People use colors to describe feelings. A sad person feels "blue." A jealous person is "green with envy."

Color in Light

We see color because of light. Light is energy that moves in waves.

The color of light depends on its **wavelength**. Red light has a long wavelength. Blue light's wavelength is short. White light contains all wavelengths.

Prisms and Rainbows

Prisms can separate white light into all the different wavelengths. Red, orange, yellow, green, blue, indigo, and violet are the colors in the **visible spectrum**.

Drops of water can act like prisms.
Raindrops can separate sunlight to make
a rainbow after a storm. Droplets of water
near waterfalls also make rainbows.

Reflecting and Absorbing Color

An object's color depends on how it **reflects** or **absorbs** light. A red apple reflects red light and absorbs all other colors. An object that reflects all light is white. A black object absorbs all the wavelengths of light.

Fun Fact!
People wear white clothing to stay cool in summer. It reflects the sun's hot light.

Mixing Color

Mixing **primary colors** makes new colors. The primary colors of light are red, blue, and green. New colors of light are made by adding wavelengths of light together.

Pigments, such as paint, can also be mixed. The primary colors of pigments are red, blue, and yellow. Mixing pigments makes new colors by reflecting or absorbing different wavelengths of light.

Fun Fact!

Mixing red and green light will make yellow light, but mixing red and green paint will make brown paint.

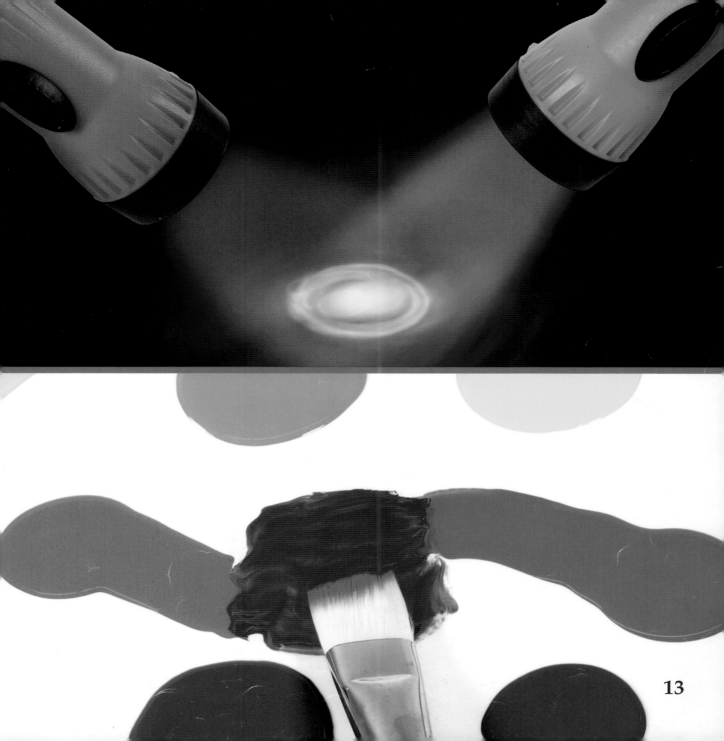

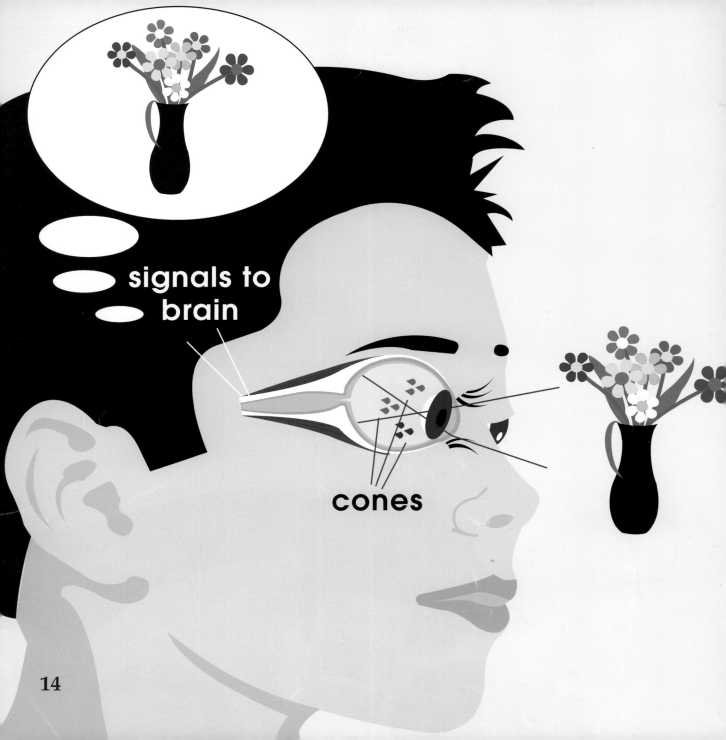

Seeing Color

People can see about 10 million colors. Our eyes have color **receptors** called cones. Cones let us see different colors. Some cones see red, some see blue, and some see green.

Our eyes turn the light they see into signals. The signals are then sent to our brains. Our brains turn the signals into the color pictures we see.

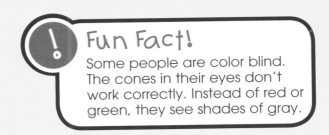

Fun Fact!
Some people are color blind. The cones in their eyes don't work correctly. Instead of red or green, they see shades of gray.

Color Warnings

Color is often used as a warning. Some animals use color to warn their enemies. Poison arrow frogs are brightly colored to show they are very poisonous.

Signs have bright colors to warn people. Red stop signs tell people to stop for traffic. Bright yellow signs tell us to stay away from dangerous areas.

René Descartes

French scientist René Descartes studied color in the 1600s. He was the first to believe that the color of an object is related to the light it reflects.

But Descartes also believed that pieces of light spin to make different colors. Now we know it is the different wavelengths of light that make color.

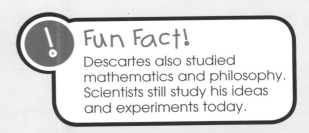

Fun Fact!
Descartes also studied mathematics and philosophy. Scientists still study his ideas and experiments today.

Different cultures name colors differently. Some languages don't have separate words for green and blue, or for yellow and orange.

The Dani of New Guinea have only two words for all colors. *Mili* is the word for all dark colors. *Mola* is the word for all light colors.

Hands On: Mixing Colors

Artists often mix paint to create the colors they want to use. You can create your own colors too.

What You Need

3 small plastic cups
red paint
blue paint
yellow paint

paper
paintbrush
bowl of water

What You Do

1. Fill one cup with red paint, one with blue paint, and one with yellow paint.
2. Paint a solid 3-inch (7.6-centimeter) square of each color on your paper. Wash the brush in the water before switching colors.
3. Now paint a different color over part of each square. Remember to wash the brush between paints. Does painting over other colors make new colors?
4. Try painting all three colors over each other. What color do they make?

Can you make all the colors of the visible spectrum? You can paint a picture with the colors you create.

Glossary

absorb (ab-ZORB)—to soak up light

pigment (PIG-muhnt)—a substance that gives color to something

primary color (PRYE-mair-ee KUHL-ur)—one of three colors which, when combined, make all colors

prism (PRIZ-uhm)—a clear object that separates light into the colors of the visible spectrum

receptor (re-CEP-tuhr)—a cell or group of cells in the eye that respond to light

reflect (ri-FLEKT)—to return light from an object

visible spectrum (VIZ-uh-buhl SPEK-truhm)—the range of colors that can be seen by the human eye

wavelength (WAYV-length)—the distance between the top of one wave of light and the top of the next wave

Read More

Hidalgo, Maria. *Color.* Let's Investigate. Mankato, Minn.: Creative Education, 2003.

Lilly, Melinda. *Color.* Read and Do Science. Vero Beach, Fla.: Rourke, 2004.

Royston, Angela. *Color.* My World of Science. Chicago: Heinemann, 2002.

Internet Sites

FactHound offers a safe, fun way to find Internet sites related to this book. All of the sites on FactHound have been researched by our staff.

Here's how:
1. Visit *www.facthound.com*
2. Type in this special code **0736854002** for age-appropriate sites. Or enter a search word related to this book for a more general search.
3. Click on the **Fetch It** button.

FactHound will fetch the best sites for you!

Index